Failing Greatly

Your Guide to Achieving Success after Failure

Dan Smith

First Printing January, 2017

Although the author and publisher have made every effort to ensure the accuracy and completeness of information contained in this book, we assume no responsibility for errors, inaccuracies, omissions, or any inconsistencies herein. Any slights of people, places, or organizations are unintentional.

ISBN – 13: 978-1542499729

ISBN -10: 1542499720

Printed in United States of America

For information contact: Dan Smith at

www.ByDanSmith.com

Cover Design: Eunicegraphicx

Editing: Rebecca's Author Services

Interior Formatting: Intention Media

Acknowledgments

I would like to thank my editor, Rebecca Camarena, for putting up with my schizophrenic slow-pace some months and get-it-done-now-pace on other days routine, my massive run-on sentences and my OCD-like fixation on certain chapters.

A big thank you is also in order for Kamila Behrens, my book coach and publicist, for making the entire process come alive and become a reality for me; Especially since I might be the worst micro-managing author she's ever had to put up with.

Of course, I owe a debt of gratitude to all the individuals mentioned throughout the book; Ron, Jeff, Tim and everyone else. Thank you for the parts you have played in my life and in helping me discover the best version of myself. Without your stories, this book would not have come to life.

Finally, and most importantly, thank you to all my readers. Really! I want to take a moment to sincerely say thank you for taking valuable time out of your hectic life to listen to the message I'm sharing.

Also by Dan Smith

Daily Victory Log

More information can be found at

www.ByDanSmith.com

What Others Are Saying About....

"Working with Dan Smith has increased my business by 20 percent each year and given me more balance to my personal life. He has been where we are and knows our struggles intimately."
Heather Gennette, The Gennette Group

"Dan's message in *Failing Greatly* is powerful! Having a balance between career and life is essential to long term success and happiness."
Lucas Smith, Black Pearl Investments

Dedication

For my most loving and supportive wife, Melody, without you this book would remain just a bucket-list idea.

For my four children Sawyer, Jonah, Tennyson and McKenna; It's the four of you who make me want to be a better person and the greatest Dad ever.

For my parents, Ken and Earline; Thank you for instilling in me the work ethic and belief system I have today.

For my brother Don; Thank you for keeping my family and I afloat during some difficult times.

Table of Contents

One

I've Been There

"Too many men are afraid of failing."

Henry Ford

Most people don't know this about Henry Ford, but his first two car companies were complete failures. It wasn't until his third attempt, named after himself, the Ford Motor Company, that he actually became a success. And not just any success. He would eventually become the third richest man alive during his time. He is most famous for using assembly lines for mass production. He implemented the eight-hour work shift three times a day instead of the ten-hour shift two times a day thus making the production more efficient and profitable while improving the lives of his workers. One of his most famous quotes is, "Failure is simply the opportunity to begin again, this time more intelligently."

Let's talk about failure. Let's go back to 2007. I was attending an annual charity event that I had participated in for nearly a decade in Irvine, California. It was not a good time in my life. I did not have the donation money to get into the event, nor did I have the money to bring toys to donate to the charity. In years past, I had written very large checks and brought trunk loads of toys. So when I told those at the door, "Oh, I'd already paid so and so," and I told the others collecting toys, "I've already given all of my toys to so and so," it was quite believable because of the level of my giving in the past.

That year I wasn't able to do any donating because of how quickly things had gone south for me. In fact, I had just enough gas in my car to make the drive, but not enough gas to get home. My car of choice was a $110,000 Mercedes Benz that was going to be re-possessed the following week. My credit cards were charged to the max or had been taken away. I had no cash. I didn't even have enough money in the bank to withdraw twenty dollars from the ATM. Until that time I wasn't aware the ATM machines didn't give $10 bills. Has that ever happened to you?

Some of you might have been or are currently in this position, and I know it's no fun at all. It's especially no fun when what you were doing just a year or two before was such a different standard and a different lifestyle.

I had gone to this event for two reasons: first, to talk with old acquaintances, friends and colleagues and second, I wanted to secure a loan or two from them to get me through the tough times. I dreamed up the scenario that somebody would invite me to lunch and I'd strike up a conversation for a loan to carry me through a few months. Then I'd be able to find someone else and say, "Oh my gosh, I forgot my wallet and my car is out of gas. Could I borrow a few dollars so I can get home?" It was planned out perfectly in my head. Unfortunately, I was unsuccessful on both fronts. My friends were not going to bail me out of the dire circumstances that I had created for myself. Never mind bailouts, no one even invited me to lunch. There were a few reasons for all this. The biggest one probably being that over the years I was sort of a jerk.

At this point, when the half-day event had ended, I had no lunch, no loans and no gas money. What I had was a car that could not make it more than a few blocks out of the parking lot because it was running on fumes. I ended up doing what I thought I would never have to do. I left the car behind and for the first time in my life, I figured out how to use public transportation in the United States. I caught a bus home, called Fletcher Jones Mercedes Benz in Newport Beach and said, "Here's where you can get your car." On the bus ride back to south Orange County I was berating myself, "How had I fallen so far? How had things gotten to this point? How was I ever going to make it out? Could I ever get back what I had? Was my situation ever going to change?"

Two years earlier, I not only owned my own company but I owned several companies. I was making over $200,000 a month. A month! Not a year, a month. Do you know how much $200,000 a month gets you? You can buy anything, do anything, go anywhere, and spend like a mad man. Believe me I spent like a mad man. I had a multi-million dollar home on the water, several cars and several boats. I chartered private planes rather than fly on commercial airliners.

My life had unfolded like the movie, *The Boiler Room* (2000) where Ben Affleck, playing the character of Jim Young, tells all the new recruits, "I have every toy imaginable." I was just like that. I had every toy imaginable. I was a professional spender. Everything you could think of and everything you could buy I bought. I was making money hand over fist and I was spending money fist over fist.

However, unlike the movie, when Affleck's character says, "And best of all kids, I'm liquid," I was not liquid. I was anything but liquid. I was heavily leveraged, but because money was coming in every month, I didn't really worry about it. But, now, the chickens had come home to roost. How had I sunk so fast?

My personal life at this point was crumbling around me even faster than my business. I was the father of three gorgeous boys, Sawyer, Jonah, and Tennyson who had moved over two hours away from me because their mother and I were divorcing. I had run most of my relationships with those I liked and loved into the ground. Sure, up until that point, I was making a ton of money, but I had absolutely no balance in my life. Then when my businesses started to falter as well, I was faced with being left with nothing.

My mindset was a total wreck and I believed that life, as I knew it, was practically over. I won't lie, that year was fantastic in terms of business and profit. I was making money and I was having fun burning through it. However, it was all one-sided; There was success in my business but not in my personal life. I didn't even understand what that meant or what the difference was at the time.

It took years for me to turn my mindset around and to start making the changes that were necessary to achieve success. But, this time, success would come in both life and business. It struck me as I started again, that I too was walking in the footsteps of Henry Ford and my failure, as was his, was simply the opportunity to begin again, however this time with a little more intelligence.

If you want to learn from someone who has failed in every possible way, then I am your guy. If you want a mentor who has experienced massive amounts of success, and then learned how to blow it, then I am your guy. If you want advice from one who's learned from life's lessons, and can now help you avoid the pitfalls, then I am your guy. Now don't get me wrong. You're still going to have to fail. You're still going to have to experience pain. However, if you'd like to lessen the failures and the pain and be able to rebound more quickly, then I am your guy.

This book is a blueprint. It's my intention for you to implement what you read and learn in this book, chapter-by-chapter, into your life and business and have success in both. I hope this book will be opened day-in and day-out, to certain chapters as needed, to remind you of ideas that can help. It is not intended to be a book to be read and put away on a shelf and never thought of again. It is a living document and it's my hope you will constantly refer to it for guidance and advice. I hope it will help you get on track for the first time or back on track. When you start to feel overwhelmed and you're not sure which direction to take next it's your blueprint for being successful in life and in business.

Notes:

Two

My Fear of Failure

"I failed my way to success."

Thomas Edison

As a boy, Thomas Edison's teacher told him he was too stupid to learn. She told him that he should just quit school and get a job. This was more than 100 years ago when not everybody went to school and some boys went into the workforce at a very early age. Imagine your teachers telling you that you were so stupid that you should just give up and get a job. Imagine them telling that to your children.

Now, obviously, we all know Thomas Edison was the one who invented the light bulb. He gave us our modern life, as we know it today because of being able to light the world. What most people don't know about Thomas Edison was that not only did he invent the light bulb, but he also filed over 1,000 other patents, and most of those did not work. His famous quote is, "I haven't failed, I've just found 10,000 ways that won't turn on a light bulb." He wasn't just failing at the light bulb. He was actually also failing at 1,000 other things during his life. He was one of the greatest inventors ever.

Ironically, in terms of experiments and ideas, he probably failed more than anyone else ever did along the way.

Fear of failure is something that has been prominent in my life. Once I had lost so much, the fear of having to go through it again if I ever rebounded was almost overwhelming. Have you ever felt that way? For me it was the fear of the pain that I had to endure. It was the fear of having everything and losing everything. It was the fear of what I would look like in front of other people. When I was making all that money, I was not shy about letting everybody know how successful I was. In retrospect, this contributed to the "jerk" reputation. The fear of having to admit how far I had fallen once, and potentially someday later having to admit it again, was something that I could not handle.

The fact that I'm sharing my story tells you that I have conquered that fear. I am able to share it and help others learn from it and I am extremely proud of that. It doesn't change the fact that I am still to this day very afraid of failure, because I know how much it hurts. The difference is I now know how to control it and use that fear to my advantage.

I was so afraid to fail again that I was frozen. I had once hung a sign in my office given to me by a good friend, Jeff Quintin from Ocean City, New Jersey. It said, "What would you do if you knew you could not fail?" When I was successful in business, I used that as my mantra. It was my guiding principle to help push me to do more and have no fear. However, once I had failed, it was an extremely difficult item to look at. In fact, it was such a painful daily reminder of my failure that I ended up throwing it away just so I wouldn't have to see it.

For years, fear of failure controlled my life. It wasn't until I got control of my fear and got control of my mindset that my life started to change for the better once again. One of the key ingredients to helping me with this change was a quote from an old friend of mine, Greg Harrelson, from South Carolina. Greg said, "I can't control the first thought that comes into my head, but I can control every thought that comes after it."

That simple idea was profound for me. I learned that crazy things come into my head. Negative and fearful thoughts of what could happen or what could go wrong. I can't control it when those thoughts come into my head, however, I can control every thought that comes after. I can change my beliefs. There is an old saying, "The mind is a scary place to go, so make sure you never go there alone." My brain was such a scary place to go to alone. Once I was able to grasp the idea of controlling my thoughts, it didn't seem as scary. Once I knew that I could control every secondary thought my life started to change almost immediately.

I know it seems a little hocus-pocus, controlling your mindset. However, the very first step in turning your life around is controlling your thoughts. Each time you have a negative or fearful thought try spending a few seconds on deciding how you can change what you're thinking about. When you have that negative or fearful thought, the first step is to realize it. The second step is to stop it right there from turning into ten negative thoughts. Then the third step is to redirect your thoughts toward something else.

Do this three-step process as often as you can when your brain sends a negative or fearful thought and you will truly start to see changes occur in your life.

Control your mindset when being negative or feeling fear:

Step 1 – Realize you are having negative thoughts

Step 2 – Stop the negative thoughts

Step 3 – Redirect your thoughts to something else

I've told you how bad that year was for me. I've shared with you how I was living an unbalanced life, placing business before family. Now, let me tell you another story about my unbalance. I was spending so much time working that I spent very little time, or practically no time, with my family. One of my most painful memories, and therefore one that I share most often, is about attending one of my son's soccer games.

Sawyer, my eldest son, was only a small child at the time. I rarely made it to any of his games or school activities because I was so busy trying to be a successful businessperson. I had arrived at one of his games, late as usual. Although the game had already started, at least he was still playing when I arrived. Of course, I wasn't focused on the game. I had three Blackberry's on me (before iPhones this was a way of communication) and I looked like Batman with all of the accessories on my belt. While I had a phone up to my ear, Sawyer did something good during the game, and I yelled out, "Great job, Sawyer!" When I think back, this was a pivotal moment in making me realize that I needed to make a change in my life. You see, what happened next was that he jogged over to his mom and said, "Mom, who's that who just yelled my name?"

Embarrassed? Guilty? A failure as a father? None of those even comes close to describing how I felt at that moment. I felt I was the kind of Dad no child wanted. I left for work in the mornings when it was dark, long before the sun came up. I came back in the evenings long after it was dark. My sons were asleep when I left. My sons were asleep when I came home. I worked six or seven days a week for years, hardly taking any family vacations. For Sawyer to see me outside of the home in my Brooks Brothers suit with my Batman accessory belt and not recognize me was earth shattering. I thought I was the perfect kind of dad trying to give my children everything they would ever want. The big problem was I hadn't realized I wasn't giving myself to them.

What kind of a dad had I become? I had zero balance in my life.

This has since changed, and I'll share with you in future chapters what changes I made and what our relationship is like today. But suffice to say, I made changes. Big changes. If there is a positive aspect to this story it's that Sawyer doesn't remember it happening. In fact, I've spent so many years since that day being so present and involved in his life that when he's heard me share this tale it seems impossible to him.

It's important for you to clearly understand that it is the choices you make, the mindset you choose to adopt, and the thought processes you follow that are going to dictate what kind of life you're going to lead. If your mindset or beliefs are important to you, but not in alignment with having balance, you, of course will then have a very unsuccessful, unbalanced life.

Notes:

Failing Greatly

Three

The Mindset Gym

"Sometimes doing our best is simply not enough.
We must do what is required."

Winston Churchill

Winston Churchill is one of my favorite sources for quotes on mindset and perseverance. Most people know Winston Churchill because he was the leader that helped Britain stand against Hitler and the Germans during World War II even when they were the only country fighting back. America and Russia had not yet entered the war and Winston Churchill kept England in the battle against the Axis powers.

One of my favorite quotes from him, and there are many, is "Success consists of going from failure to failure without loss of enthusiasm." The Churchill War Rooms is a spot in London where I believe every tourist should visit. It is close to the Houses of Parliament, Buckingham Palace and Big Ben.

Here, they have preserved the bunkers that Churchill would retire to each evening as the Nazis were about to bomb London. He lived in these war rooms, underground in the evenings, for years while leading his fellow citizens and inspiring them to continue to fight the good fight. If anyone knew anything about having a strong mindset in the face of adversity and overcoming a fear of failure, it was Churchill. Because if he failed and Great Britain lost the war, what would it mean for the country? If anyone knew what it took to build a strong mindset, and keep it, it was Winston Churchill.

How do you get a strong mindset? How do you grow those mindset muscles? In that question lies the answer. If you want to be strong physically, what do you do? You eat healthy and you exercise regularly. You go to the gym, run, do yoga, etc.

What do you do to increase your mindset muscle? Like your biceps or quadriceps, your mind is a muscle. How often do you go to the gym to work on your body? How often do you go to the mindset gym to work on your mind? You need to feed it good nutritional content. You need to exercise it regularly to strengthen the muscles.

I have this picture in my head of a strong mindset being like a brick wall. It will be almost unbreakable. On the other hand, I imagine a week mindset being made out of paper. It will be very fragile.

Picture a group of high school football players running onto the field to start a game. What do most high school football teams do? They run full-speed onto the field tearing through some sort of a paper banner the cheerleaders have made. That paper rips apart and puts up no resistance to the players as they tear through it. This is how I view a weak mindset. It puts up little to no resistance to pressure or adversity.

Now picture a tall and stout brick wall. Imagine what would happen if the players took the field and tried to run through it at full-speed. They'd just bounce off, barely causing any damage to the wall at all, right? This is how I view a strong mindset. It is able to withstand blow after blow of bad news or failures without tumbling down.

Your mindset has to be like that brick wall. So how do you make your wall strong? You work on three things: building it higher, wider and deeper. How do you make your mindset strong? You go to the mindset gym.

People ask me all the time when I talk about the mindset gym, "Dan, where is this gym? Where do I go? What kind of machines do I use?" Ok, fine, no one actually asks that silly of a question, but you get the point of what I'm trying to get across. When we go to an actual gym, we have the use of weight machines and cardio machines. Some gyms have swimming pools, basketball courts and even boxing rings. Spin, Pilates, Cross-fit, Boot-Camp, the list goes on and on. There are so many options available to us to work on our bodies yet almost no attention is given to our minds.

Let me give you some examples of the equipment available for you to use to work out your mindset. Following are the pieces of equipment that I use.

First is the use of affirmations, sometimes referred to as self-talk. Now, I know some of you think these are incredibly corny. In fact, I also thought that way before I started doing them and truly understood their value. I've found it much easier to do them alone (it still feels a bit corny doing them in front of others), loudly and with music playing in the background. Corny or not, there is no denying that saying powerful things with energy and enthusiasm will in turn

17

make you feel more powerful, energetic and enthusiastic. Ralph Waldo Emerson once said, "Nothing great was ever achieved without enthusiasm." And even if it makes you feel just the tiniest bit more powerful, energetic and enthusiastic, then it was worth it, wouldn't you agree? As you do them more and more, day after day, you will begin to see the changes go from tiny to dramatic.

Another piece of mindset gym equipment available to us is YouTube. Try typing in the word motivation or inspiration. Currently, over seven million videos are available under motivation. You don't have to get creative to find motivation or inspiration on YouTube. Don't use the excuse I didn't know how to look for it or I didn't know what to type in. Simply type in either the words *inspire, inspiration, motivate* or *motivation,* and you will have a lifetime of choices to watch.

One of my personal favorite pieces of equipment in the mindset gym is an oldie but goodie, books. "Reading" books in the twenty-first century can be done in several ways; paper, digital or audio. I'd encourage you choose what best works for you. Some, myself included, still read paper books the old-fashioned way. Others prefer the convenience of using their pads or some other sort of device. And still others seem to absorb information best by listening to audio books. Personally, I fall asleep if I listen to a book on audio and just can't stand reading on my iPad. But that's me. You've got to figure out what works best for you.

Lets not forget the original piece of mindset gym equipment, a journal. Studies have taught us that as human beings we process information and absorb messages best when writing them down. So consider keeping a journal. I have had great success over the years keeping what I call a "Victory Log." What is that?

First, you don't need any fancy equipment. You only need a pen or pencil and some paper. Personally, I prefer $.99 composition books, the kind you used in high school or college. Of course, there is nothing wrong with a nice $29.99 leather journal from Barnes & Noble or either. The choice is yours.

I try to write in my "Victory Log" at the end of each day or in the evening before going to sleep. I'll tell you why in just a bit. It's a simple process. I'm not looking to write a term paper each day covering all the things that happened. I don't want it to be a 20-minute chore. It's intended to be a three-minute exercise. I simply take a moment to focus and try to recall all the small victories I achieved during that day. There should be nothing negative and no complaints. It's just a log of my victories throughout the day. They could be as small and simple as getting to the gym (the actual gym) on time in the morning to following my nutrition plan throughout the day to having one of my kids tell me they love me. They could be as big and eventful as scheduling a big trip to speak to audiences in several cities to buying another investment property to celebrating another anniversary with my wife. All victories, the small ones, the big ones and all the ones in-between, go into the log. By recording these victories on a consistent basis, you're retraining your brain to focus on the positive, not the negative. Try it for a few weeks and you'll notice a difference in your outlook, I guarantee it.

There you have it. All the equipment you need to start going to the mindset gym and strengthening your mindset muscles. Do these simple exercises and you'll begin to see instant results, just like at the real gym. Now that you know what to do, the challenge, just as it is with the real gym, is figuring out the when to do. Here are my suggestions:

- Start your day doing affirmations. Two to three minutes is all it will take to get your mindset going in the right direction to start your day off powerfully, energetically and with enthusiasm.

- Squeeze in five to ten minutes to read something powerful in whatever format you've chosen and another five to ten minutes at some other time to watch something powerful on YouTube. Use lunch breaks or your commute or whenever you can work it in to your schedule.

- Keep a "Victory Log" each evening before going to sleep. Three to five minutes of focused thought about all the good that happened to you that day. Going to sleep with those victories being the last thing you think of, and having written them down will help you sleep better and wake up more fresh. That's how our subconscious works.

Most of us have joined a gym after New Years at the beginning of the year. Most of us have tried to stick to a diet or a food plan. And most of us, even after seeing positive results from the exercise or nutrition plan, fall back into our old habits within a matter of months, sometimes weeks. If you really want to accomplish something big, you've got to stick with it. Consistency is the key to developing a new habit. You must persevere through the adversity and distractions and all the noise around you. Most importantly, when you fail at doing what you were supposed to do, don't dwell on it and continue to fail. Fix the problem right then and there and begin doing what you are supposed to again at that moment.

Receive your free one-week sample of the *Daily Victory Log* by going to the author's website.

www.ByDanSmith.com

Notes:

Four

The Worst-Case Scenario Game

"The only thing we have to fear is fear itself."

Franklin D. Roosevelt

This chapter is very intense. "The-Worst Case Scenario" game is a mind game in the arsenal of your mindset toolbox. It was an invaluable tool in teaching me what I feared. In terms of failure, there isn't much to be afraid of compared to what the worst-case scenario could be. Once you lose that fear of failure, once you no longer think that things are as bad as they can get, you realize that it's okay to fail. You realize that things can get better and are already better than just about any worst-case scenarios.

In the movie *After Earth* (2016) Will Smith's character, Cypher Raige, had an incredible perspective on fear while talking to his son about a traumatic moment. He says something along the lines of fear is not real and the only place that fear can exist is in our thoughts of the future. He explains that fear is simply a product of our imagination causing us to fear things that do not at present and may not ever exist. He goes on a bit later to tell his son to not misunderstand him because danger is very real. But fear is a choice. Daily we have to confront our fears, even when facing a worst-case scenario.

Let's play the "Worst-Case Scenario" game. Again, thanks are due to my good friend, Jeff Quintin, for teaching me. Be warned. It is a very difficult game to play. Even now, as I write these words, I am on edge. That's how powerful a tool this is that I'm sharing with you. Take a situation in your life that you are currently struggling with, afraid of, or having difficulty with. It could be personal. It could be financial. It could be a relationship. It could be in business. While you may, and probably do, have more than just one item that is stressing you out, to play this game correctly choose just one problem to start with. For purposes of an example, let's choose something very general that most of us can probably relate to.

Not making enough money is something you may fear. What do you fear about that? It could mean no longer paying for your current standard of housing, be it a mortgage or rent. Maybe you can no longer make your current car payments. Perhaps your credit cards have been closed because you were not making the minimum payments or had maxed them to the limit. That could mean that now you have to move to a smaller home or get a lesser quality car.

Yeah, that seems scary but is it really the worst-case scenario? No, not really! Now, check this out! How about having the sheriff come to your door to move the stuff out of the home that you're losing or getting evicted from because you had no money? That would, obviously, be a worse worst case, wouldn't it? How about having to admit to your family and friends that you've lost your great car, have no money to get a lesser car and are now having to rely on public transportation. That would be an even worse case, right? How about having to admit to your family that you have no more credit cards and no money so no longer would you be able to go to McDonald's or the toy store. It would be even worse when it was time buy important things like school supplies or clothes if there was no money was available to buy them. Isn't that a much bigger worst case?

Is that the absolute worst case? I don't think so. Take it even further and you can begin to see how this game works. You truly take everything to it's extreme. It's tough to give an example of going to the worst-case extreme for everyone reading this book, but that's what I'm trying to accomplish. Remember, this is just an example and yours will be different in so many ways.

Since you've been evicted and you're homeless, where do you go? Can you go to an American Red Cross shelter? Or perhaps even to the basement of some church shelter for the needy? Would this be worst case? Since you can't drive anywhere in your own car and have to rely on public transportation, what about your kids? You don't really have a permanent physical address, so do your kids have to drop out of school? Worst case? Not yet. How are you going to eat and feed your family if you have no job, no money and no way to get around? Would you have to be like those people you see at the corner of all the Costco's around the United States, holding up a sign asking for spare change? Would this be a more worst case? Of course, it would.

Starts to get kind of ugly, doesn't it? Suddenly having a little less money doesn't seem so bad, does it? This is just one example. Imagine if you played this game in all areas of your life where you're afraid of things going wrong. Perhaps, ending up in a homeless shelter, having to buy clothes from the Goodwill, and having to panhandle would be your worst-case scenario due to losing your job. What is truly frightening for you is how this would affect you and your family.

Here is where I start to get philosophical on you. Are you still healthy? Is your family still healthy? Do you still love your kids? More importantly, do your kids still love you? Do you still have a faith in something greater? While the picture I painted a few minutes ago is grim, believe me, there are thousands of families out there in the world today who still wished they could live that life. To live with their loved ones, even in a shelter and having to panhandle, but still together as a family with everyone healthy. True worst-case scenario could mean, you, or even worse yet, your loved ones losing their good health. How bad would that be? What if your kids no longer loved you? How bad would that be? Even as I write this, I know it's going to offend some of you, but I want you to understand the premise of this exercise. God forbid your children were to pass away, how bad would that be? Suddenly, your prior worst case doesn't seem so bad, does it? In comparison, you would probably trade everything to keep your family healthy, loving, and together. Wouldn't you?

Playing the worst-case scenario game helps us to see that even if things seem to be bad and we get stressed out, they are not as bad as they could be. It's a matter of having perspective. Even if it got ten times worse than it is today, it's still probably a lot better than how it could potentially be if we took it all the way down that road, isn't it?

By comparing the current supposed worst case to the absolutely, unthinkable worst case, we can stop feeling sorry for ourselves. We can stop worrying about how bad things are, realizing that they are not really that bad after all. Instead, we can use that wasted energy and emotion to create a better life for ourselves and for those around us. This exercise is brutal but intended to change our focus about our current situation.

Notes:

Five

Success, Inch-by-Inch

"Success is not a big step in the future; Success is a small step taken right now."

Jonatan Martensson

Now that we have gotten control of our mindsets, we are better able to control our thoughts and our emotions, so we can move forward with progressing on the blueprint for success. The first step in this blueprint, to be a success in life and business, was getting control of our heads. In previous chapters, we have learned how to do that. Don't get me wrong. It won't happen for you as quick as the thirty minutes it took to read the last four chapters. It is going to be a constant struggle, day-in and day-out, for the rest of your life because we always have something happening around us or to us. We always have something or someone attacking our brick wall mindset. But now, you're prepared for it and know a few ways to help deal with the challenges and adversity.

In the movie, *Any Given Sunday*, (1999) Al Pacino plays the role of football coach Tony D'Amato. The most poignant scene of the movie is of him giving one last talk to his team before they hit the field. View the clip of *Any Given Sunday* at the author's YouTube page: www.youtube.com/c/dansmithusa

Some key parts of his message to the team:

- "We're in hell right now gentleman. Believe me. And we can stay here, get the sh*t kicked out of us, or we can fight our way back, into the light. We can climb out of hell, one inch at a time."

- You know, when you get old, in life things get taken from you. I mean that's, that's part of life. But you only learn that when you start losing stuff. You find out life's this game of inches, and so is football. Because in either game, life or football, the margin for error is so small. I mean, one-half a step too late or too early and you don't quite make it. One-half second to slow or too fast, you don't quite catch it. The inches we need are everywhere around us. They're in every break in the game, every minute, every second.

- On this team, we fight for that inch. On this team, we tear ourselves and everyone else around us to pieces for that inch. We claw with our fingernails for that inch. Because we know when we add up all those inches that's going to make the f**king difference between winning and losing. Between living and dying. I'll tell you this, in any fight it's the guy whose willing to die who's going to win that inch, and I know that if I'm going to have any life anymore it's because I'm still willing to fight and die for that inch. Because that's what living is. The six inches in front of your face.

A friend, Riley Sullivan from Victorville, California shared this powerful scene with me. Watching the four-minute clip on YouTube for the first time was a life-changing moment for me.

I know that might seem cliché, and maybe even a little odd, but the message resonated with me as nothing ever had. I knew instantly that the monologue would be instrumental for the rest of my life in making me realize something very important; That life is a game of inches. Nothing happens overnight. It takes time. Anything worthwhile takes time. Everything is accomplished inch-by-inch.

In our blueprint of being able to move forward, to have success in both life and business, it is paramount that we understand there is no such thing as an overnight success. We will not see dramatic changes by just reading three chapters or doing something consistently for four days or even four weeks. It will happen, but it will happen inch-by-inch.

I'd like to share a story with you about inch-by-inch growth and improvement. It's my inch-by-inch story covering the years 2011 through 2016, a six-year period-of-time. I finally started to get control of my mindset in 2011. It's when I started to fight my way back, into the light, and I started to climb out of Hell, one inch at a time.

The first inch forward occurred at the beginning of 2011 when an old friend, John Carmody, of Big Bear Lake, California, asked me to begin coaching him. John is a real estate agent, and real estate in 2011 was particularly difficult after the subprime mortgage meltdown that completely ruined the real estate industry and the U.S. economy in general. So in the beginning of 2011 I took my first step forward, my first inch, and began coaching John.

After a few months, and with John starting to have more success, he also asked me to coach his team. My first inch was coaching someone and doing something productive and helpful. My second inch I was helping not only John, but also an entire team.

Another friend, Laura Ford from Mission Viejo, California, asked me to do the same. However, I declined. I told her it wasn't what I "really" did and I was just doing it to help out John. This is a great example of the inches we need that are all around us. It was there for me to take. I just couldn't see it. My mindset was starting to get better, but it wasn't strong yet. I missed the opportunity. It was right there, six inches in front of my face, but I didn't quite catch it.

A few months later John introduced me to one of his friends, Lauri Strain from the San Luis Obispo area of California, who also wanted help and coaching in real estate. This time, I saw the opportunity. I grabbed the inch and began coaching her. Now I had clients. Plural. That was inch number three. I decided to start a coaching company and that became inch number four. This all happened over a ten-month period, not overnight.

It was at this point I began to meet some resistance to my newfound success and stronger mindset. Has that ever happened to you; you start to turn things around and life tries to throw something to derail the success? My resistance came in the form of other established coaches and trainers with their cease and desist orders and lawsuit threats. It seemed they didn't want another competitor. The lawsuits never occurred, being they were completely baseless, but the entire ordeal was still distracting and a bit unnerving. I did not recognize it at the time, but that was another pivotal moment for my mindset. Two outcomes could have occurred. Either I could've taken that adversity and backed down and given up or I could've faced it and beat it down. Fortunately, I decided to do the latter. I fought for that inch. I clawed, with my fingernails, for that inch. Looking back it's easy to see that had I withdrawn, my entire life today would be different, and probably not for the better. Thankfully, I took a stand and persevered through the adversity. Pushing on was my next inch forward.

And when I did, would you believe that another inch presented itself? A 40-office real estate company approached me to coach their agents. This was my first exposure to public speaking and as it turned out, I was very poor at it. But the opportunity was a pretty big step, and another inch in the right direction. It was outside of my comfort zone, but a necessary step to continue making progress. Over the course of six months, speaking once or twice a month to audiences between 15 and 20 agents, I began to become more skilled in the art of speaking. 17 months from the start of 2011, the inches were starting to pile up and they were making a difference.

The next inch came as I moved into a new rental home. It was May of 2012. Years before, during my meltdown, I had foreclosed all my homes. Since then I had been rental hopping. It turned out my newest landlord was a business partner with Dave Huey, from Seattle, Washington, the founder of a company, Sound Equity.

Coincidentally, Sound Equity had just launched a new product and was looking for someone to present it to real estate agents across all of Southern California.

What amazing timing, right? The inches are everywhere around us. We just need to see them and act. One of my first mentors, Tim Wood from Big Bear Lake, California, once told me, "Good luck is simply being prepared when an opportunity arises." I wasn't prepared when Laura had asked me to coach her, but I was prepared this time to grab on to that inch.

I began to present and train real estate agents all over the region. I was on the road three or four times a week speaking to audiences between 50 and 100 people. While the 40-office real estate company helped me become better, it was this opportunity that allowed me to master the art of public speaking. After speaking to hundreds of audiences and thousands of people, I learned how to read an audience. I learned what it took to make everyone in the room laugh and what it took to make everyone in the room cry. Dave has become a good friend in the years since and I still owe him for the opportunity he gave me.

Interestingly, I couldn't have taken advantage of this opportunity, this inch, without all of the prior inches. Had I tried to take this step back in the beginning, when I was only working with John, it would not have been an inch; It would've been like crossing the Grand Canyon, impossible. I first had to learn to speak effectively to individuals, then to small groups of 15 to 20 and that allowed me to move up to audiences of 50 to 100. That set me up to take yet another inch along the path of success.

In 2013, I began hosting my own events as a public speaker. Over the years, I have spoken to audiences approaching 1,000 people. Inch-by-inch, I was making slow and steady progress.

Two years later, in 2015, I found another inch. I ran across someone who gave me with the opportunity to write this book which would lead to presenting keynote speeches to even larger and more diverse audiences not only across the U.S. but worldwide.

Lets look at all the inches over that six-year period of time:

- John Carmody
- Team Carmody
- Missed the inch with Laura Ford
- Lauri Strain
- Started a coaching company
- 40-office real estate company coaching
- New product presentations across the region
- Hosted own events
- Author and worldwide speaker

Now, check this out! This is just one of the inch-by-inch stories I could tell you about that happened to me. There are also inch-by-inch stories about my amazing relationships with my children and about meeting and marrying my inspiring soul-mate and wife, and about my financial health. The list goes on and on.

How about you? What do you want to accomplish, inch-by-inch?

Do you want to lose weight? How many pounds? It's going to be a struggle and it's going to take discipline and it's going to take persistence and it's going to take a consistent effort. To lose a substantial amount of weight a person has to eat healthy and exercise regularly. Do the work inch-by-inch, and you'll lose the waistline, inch-by-inch.

Do you want to have a better relationship with your significant other? Maybe with your children? Improving relationships doesn't happen overnight. In fact, all things worthwhile tend to be rather difficult and take time. There is an old saying that I really love, "I didn't say it was going to be easy; I said it was going to be worth it." Improving personal relationships takes time, effort, and work. Inch-by-inch, day-by-day, it gets better and better. Even when it's great, inch-by-inch, it can get even greater.

You want to make more sales or get a promotion or make partner? You must realize by now, it won't happen overnight. It's going to take steps, difficult steps, over a period of time, inch-by-inch, to accomplish what needs to be done to make that happen. You don't just get to show up for work and do a good job and four weeks later hit the big time. No one starts at the top. It happens inch-by-inch.

What are your stories? Are you prepared to start improving things in your life, inch-by-inch? It all starts with the first step, that first inch.

Notes:

Six

The Pyramid

"Setting a goal is not the main thing. It is deciding how you will go about achieving it and staying with that plan."

Tom Landry

Over the years, I've learned some really great ideas from some really great sources and put them all together to make what I consider the most concise, easy to read, and complete goal setting and business planning system there is. I'd like to share it now. I call it *The Pyramid*. It has seven stages, or levels, to it; *The Dreams, The Goals, The Plans, The Activities, The Schedule, Tracking,* and *Accountability*. We will go over each stage one-by-one on the following pages. Best of all, we'll have illustrations. Please follow along, level-by-level. Obviously, in the real world we would use a bigger piece of paper or even a small poster board for *The Pyramid*. It would be something to carry with us or hang somewhere to see it daily. What it wouldn't be is another lost idea stuck in a drawer, never touched or evaluated throughout the year.

Have you ever made a gigantic, thorough business plan that was about 12 pages long? Was it full of everything imaginable that was going to go on in either your business or your life for the coming year? I've made those kinds of plans before. Then did it get stuck in the drawer, and halfway through the year you couldn't remember what goals you'd set or what plans you'd made? Heck, you couldn't even remember putting it in the drawer? I've done that too. Obviously, if we don't know what goals we've set or plans we've made then we don't know if we're achieving them. We don't know how far ahead of pace or behind pace we are. The purpose of *The Pyramid* is to make keeping the information accessible. We should be able to look at it and give ourselves a report card, a quick checkup on a regular basis to see where we stand in relation to where we should be.

The Pyramid should be used in both life and business for setting goals and making the plans to achieve them.

The Dreams

Following is an illustration of *The Pyramid* (Yes, it definitely resembles a triangle). Notice, there is a line down the center with the left-hand side labeled "Life" and the right-hand side labeled "Business/Financial." Also, notice the line going from left to right forming our top level labeled *The Dreams*. *The Dreams* is at the top for a reason. It is where we finally want to end up at in life once we've made it. If we've achieved success in life and in business, what does that look like? How do you define it? Imagine that you have made it to the top. You have everything you want. You've done everything you wanted to do. Paint a picture in your head.

Start writing those things on *The Pyramid* on the next page for your personal and business life.

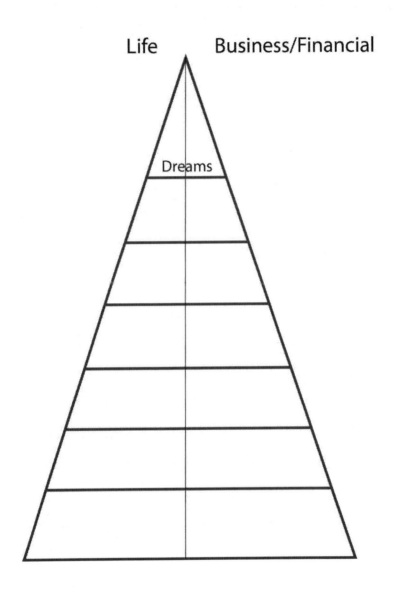

What does your life look like once you've made it? I've found that a lot of people put ideas such as the following:

- I'm healthy
- I'm wealthy
- I'm able to enjoy life

While all of the above sound good, they need some work. Timothy Ferriss, author of *The 4-Hour Workweek* does a great job of explaining how to set goals. It's a terrific book. Unfortunately, I believe 99.9% of us can't get away with a four-hour workweek like he does as we don't do something quite as automated as he explained in the book. However, that's not to say a lot can't be learned from it. It is a definite suggested read on my Top Ten list; Specifically, chapter four. His ideas on goal setting I found very valuable. I've shared his ideas with others and they have also found them very helpful in determining the importance of their goals and what their goals should actually be. I'm not going to give away his secrets. Buy the book. And implement his three steps to figure out what is really important to you and how you should plan for more clear and concise ambitions or goals.

Speaking of clear and concise goals, the examples I gave above are neither. They are the typical ones I hear people give, but then again, most people don't typically achieve their goals. For a goal to be achieved it has to be clear and concise and there has to be a plan of action to make it happen. Simply writing down that you want something isn't enough. It won't just miraculously occur. You've probably realized that by now with some of your unachieved goals and dreams.

Be specific.

- I'm healthy is not specific enough. I will weigh 165 pounds, have body fat of 15% or less, and be able to run a six-minute mile is somewhat specific, but could be even more so.

- I'm wealthy is not specific enough. I will have a net worth of $5,000,000, have monthly residual income of $25,000 and have no debt is somewhat specific, but could be even more so.

- I'm able to enjoy life is not specific enough. I will take a week-long vacation each quarter to a different country each time, drive my dream car which is a Land Rover Defender, and be able to volunteer weekly in my children's or grandchildren's classrooms is somewhat specific, but could be even more so.

Take an hour or two and work on filling in the top of *The Pyramid* with very specific dreams. These are our definitions of success so they are definitely worth taking the time to think about and put down on paper. And trust me, it is going to be something you're constantly working on and making changes to. Your dreams today probably won't be exactly the same as your dreams a year or two from now. Life changes. The things that are important to us sometimes change. Our priorities sometimes change. This is a living, breathing, and fluid plan that we're constantly looking at and making adjustments to.

The Goals

Now that we have the first level of *The Pyramid* more clearly identified, we can move on to the next.

The second level of *The Pyramid* is labeled *The Goals*. Here's something very important you must remember. *The Goals* are simply the stepping-stones to achieving *The Dreams*. If one of your dreams on the personal side was to lose 20 pounds then your goals are your stepping-stones for getting there. You don't just lose 20-pounds at once in a week. You lose one or two pounds in a week. You lose five or six pounds in a month. Now you have a goal for the week. Now you have a goal for the month. Eventually, step-by-step, inch-by-inch, you achieve the dream of losing 20 pounds and reaching your ultimate goal.

If your dream is to someday be a CEO, your goal isn't to be promoted next week. You might first want to be recognized as managerial material. You might then want to become vice president of some department. You might then become the CFO or COO. Those could be some goals, or stepping-stones, along the way to finally achieving the dream of becoming a CEO.

If you have a financial dream to buy 20 rental properties, you wouldn't want to wait to save up the money and buy all 20 on the exact same day to achieve it. In the first year, you might buy one or two. In another year, you might buy two or three. Eventually, you'll get to 20, step-by-step and inch-by-inch. This is what I mean by stepping-stones.

Take a few minutes to write your one-year goals down on *The Pyramid*. Remember, life goals on the left, business/financial goals on the right. These goals should be steps taken toward achieving *The Dreams*.

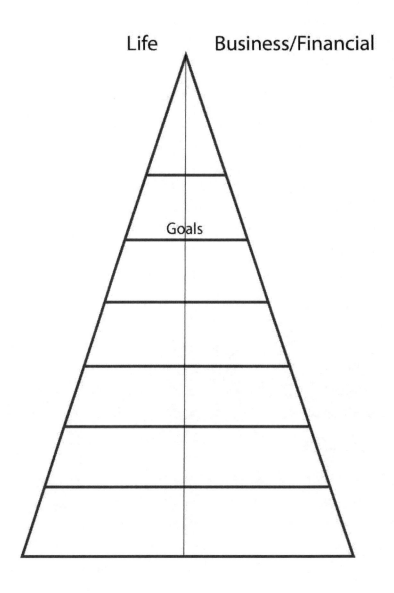

Life   Business/Financial

Goals

Earlier I mentioned that your dreams will change as life happens. Well, so will your goals along the way, even much more so. It's important to have goals for one, three, five, seven and ten years planned out in advance, but don't be afraid to change them as needed. It helps to have a road map to reach our destination and to achieve our dreams, but you also need to be aware you'll hit some speed bumps and detours along the way. And sometimes your destination, your dreams, will change altogether. That means all of your goals in relation to that dream change too, obviously. So it's much more important to focus on the now goals than the future goals. Sort of like in sports, you don't need to worry about the game next month nearly as much as you do about the game this week. You need to have three, five, seven and ten year goals, but they mean little if you can't accomplish this year's goals

Another important thing to remember about goal setting is that we tend to overestimate what we can accomplish in one year and underestimate what we can accomplish in five years. I've heard that from dozens of very smart people over the years. And it's very true. So remember, you're doing this step-by-step, inch-by-inch. Remember this as you make your goals.

The Plans and The Activities

This is where the planning part of *The Pyramid* starts to get a little difficult for many of people. Up until now, it's been pretty fun writing down your dreams and goals. However, when you have to start writing down the work required to make those things happen, that's a different story. For purposes of understanding the subtle differences between levels three and four of *The Pyramid*, labeled *The Plans* and *The Activities*. I'm going to explain them simultaneously. Many people have a tendency to get these two steps confused. I've learned that explaining them at the same time helps.

The Plans, level three of the Pyramid, is sort of our 30,000 foot, very general view of what needs to be done. *The Activities*, level four, is our list of very specific actions to be taken. Here are some examples.

If you had a dream to weigh 160 pounds and you had a goal to lose 20 pounds this year, *The Plans* section of *The Pyramid* would be to eat healthy and exercise regularly. It's a very general overview of what will be required to achieve our goal. *The Activities* section would then be very specific with steps such as to eat no more than 1,500 calories a day with one cheat day a week and to work out at the gym four times a week for at least 30 minutes. Can you see the difference? One reminds you what you need to do in general to accomplish the goal and the other lays it out in very specific steps.

Remember, for each dream there needs to be a stepping-stone or goal along the way. For each goal, there must be a basic or general plan. For each plan, there must be specific activities to accomplish.

Take some time to work on your plans and activities on *The Pyramid* on the following pages.

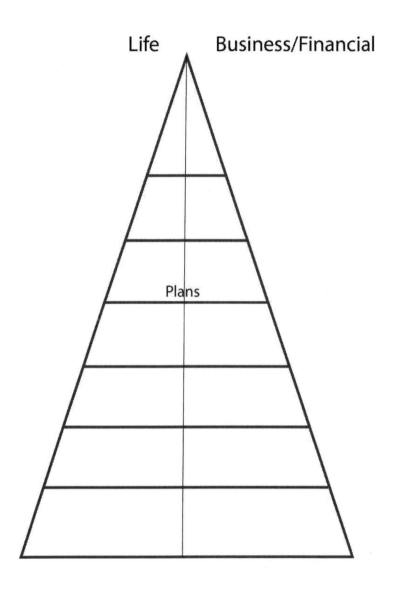

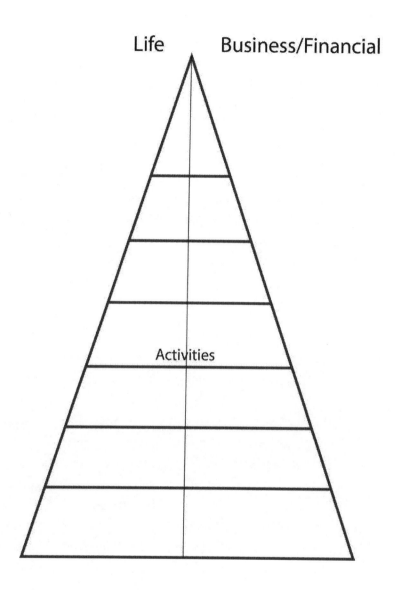

Good job! Two more levels of *The Pyramid* have progressed. You're making great strides now. Just remember, nothing worth doing is ever easy. This plan will take time and effort to complete, but aren't your dreams worth it?

The Schedule

Next, is the fifth level of *The Pyramid*, *The Schedule*. Writing our dreams and goals was fun and exciting. Writing our plans and activities was much less so because it reminded us of all the steps it will take to make everything happen. And now, you have to find a way to schedule in all of the stuff you just wrote down into your busy and hectic life.

For purposes of being consistent, let's use the same example of losing 20 lbs. You know that the plan called for eating healthy and regular exercise. You know that your activity was calorie counting, cheat days and hitting the gym a certain number of days for a certain amount of time each week. *The Schedule* level is where you will plan when you will actually complete *The Activities*. Meaning, what days and what times will you be at the gym? Are you going to try to eat regularly six times a day mixing meals and snacks as most health gurus now suggest? If so, what times are you going to have these meals and snacks? If this seem very difficult to do, it's because it is. It's going to take a lot of thought and planning. Remember, lots of thought and planning is exactly what it takes to achieve what you want. It's never going to just happen on its own.

On the following page, take your first shot and schedule in all of your listed activities from the fourth level of *The Pyramid*. I say first shot because this one will most definitely require a bit of trial and error to find out what is realistic and doable.

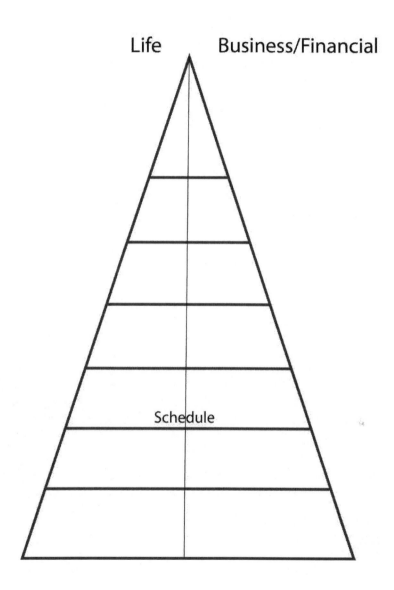

Did you notice it seemed that there were not be enough hours in the day to achieve what you wanted to do? Believe it or not that's a good thing. It makes you streamline your goals in life and business. It makes you choose the truly important ones because there's only so many hours in the day and you can only get so much done. The things you really want to do will be the ones you make time for and that stay on the list.

Tracking

We are almost to the bottom of *The Pyramid*. Only two parts left. Next, we have the sixth level, *Tracking*. As with *The Schedule* level, this section has proven to be very difficult for many people. Here's an interesting fact though. There is a direct correlation between those who have mastered the ability to do the tracking and their success versus those who found the tracking too difficult to do and therefore continued to struggle. Ask yourself, which one do you want? Success or struggle? Are you willing to track it if it means success?

What do you track? Simple. Everything. But, specifically, you should track whether or not you followed *The Schedule* to complete *The Activities*.

Tracking is a report card for you. It helps paint a picture of your efficiencies and inefficiencies in terms of following *The Schedule* to complete *The Activities* on *The Plans* to achieve *The Goals* that will ultimately lead to you reaching *The Dreams*.

On the next page, take a few moments to write down ways you could track whether or not you did what you were supposed to do from the levels above on *The Pyramid*.

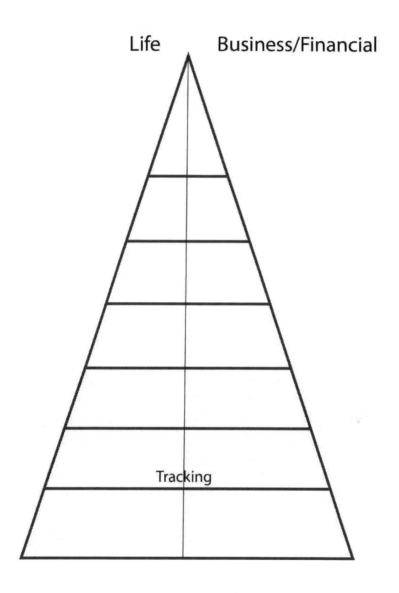

Fantastic! You've taken a giant step toward success. Successful people track just about everything; both in their lives and in their businesses. If you are not tracking how you spend your time, your energy, and your dollars, then how can you tell what you are getting for your time, for your energy, and for your dollars? You have no way to tell what is working and what is not or how well it is working. There is no way to tell what you should be doing more of and you should be doing less of. You have no way to tell what you should consider spending more on and spending less on.

You must think about your life and business and your definitions of success for both. You must refer back to *The Dreams* for this and determine what you need to track so you can review the information and begin making decisions and changes not because of a guess or a gut feel, but because of actually knowing.

Accountability

You have made it to the bottom of *The Pyramid*, level seven, *Accountability*. Look at *The Pyramid* (as though it were a structure or building, not just a triangle). Notice the bottom level is the widest part of the structure. It's the widest meaning it's also the sturdiest, and the strongest. This level supports everything above it.

This seventh level of *The Pyramid* is just like the foundation of a building. It is the foundation. It is the foundation for your dreams and goals. The foundation holds the weight and supports everything above it. Without a strong foundation, a building would crumble. Without a strong foundation, success for you in life and business will be elusive and hard to achieve.

Accountability is a nasty, ugly, four-letter word for many people. Left to their own devices, people usually take the easy way out. They usually prefer the path of least resistance, even if the path takes them in the wrong direction. *Accountability* helps prevent that.

Accountability means doing the things you don't want to do, especially on the days you don't want to do them, because you know by doing those things, day-by-day, inch-by-inch, you will achieve what you set out to achieve. You will get what you want out of this life. You will get to the level of success you want in business. *Accountability* does that.

How do you hold yourself accountable? If you can't rely solely on yourself to do all that you've set out to do, who can help you? At the gym, you may have a workout buddy. You need an accountability partner as well. Some people use their bosses, others their employees and still others co-workers.

Family can be a great accountability partner. A great friend, Pablo Rener from Newport Beach, California uses his family as his accountability partners. Imagine going home to your significant other at night and having to report in; "Yes, I did what I said I was going to do," or, "No, I did not do what I said I was going to do." Imagine having to go home and report to your children, "Yes, I did what I was supposed to do at work today," or, "No, I did not do what I was supposed to do at work today." Wow, that is being accountable. Imagine telling your daughter you couldn't take the dream trip she wanted to go on or telling your son that you couldn't buy the tickets to the game he wanted to see, because each day you came home and hadn't accomplish what you had said you were going to do. That's how Pablo does his accountability with his family. Are you brave enough to be accountable to your family?

On this level of *The Pyramid*, write down some of the ways that you could be held accountable so that you complete all the great things you've written so far.

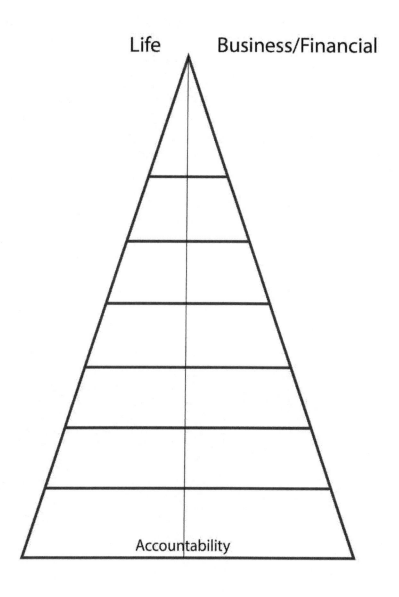

Accountability can be painful. Having to admit that we didn't do what we said we were going to do can be extremely difficult, yet it is so important. Without *Accountability*, you are setting yourself up for failure. *Accountability* is at the bottom of *The Pyramid* for a reason. As the foundation it's the most important.

There you have it, *The Pyramid*, top to bottom, all seven levels. This is how your life will look if you actually achieve everything that you want.

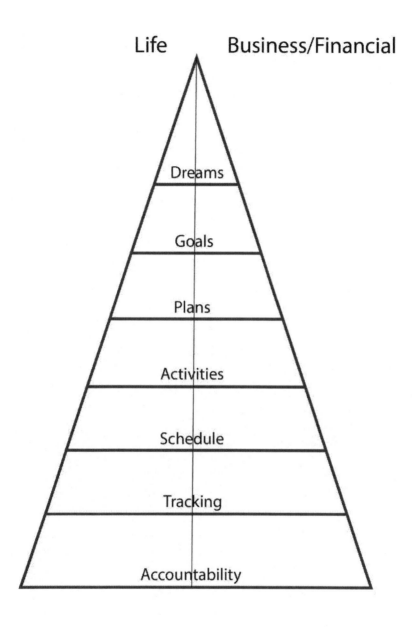

Receive your free copy of Dan's personal *Pyramid* by going to the author's website.

www.ByDanSmith.com

Notes:

Seven

Change

"Fear to change is the enemy of success."

Bhagwan Maurya

A previous mentor, Neil Schwartz from Beverly Hills, California, has a saying that he is famous for. "You are where you are in life because you're okay with it. If you weren't, you'd change." Neil is the owner of *Century 21 Masters* and is one of the most successful real estate brokers in the United States.

When you talk about being okay with where you're at and not changing, he is the perfect example. Actually, he's the perfect example of not doing it that way because he's done the opposite. So he's still a great example, in the correct sort of way. As successful as he's been for nearly two decades, I have watched from a far as he has made bold moves to expand his business dramatically. Most of us would have considered where he was to be the definition of successful, living in complete comfort and financial security. Imagine owning luxury cars, living in a Beverly Hills mansion, sending your children to Ivy League schools and having no debt. How's that for a dream? However, he thought he could accomplish more, so he continued to make changes. Let us look at what he has accomplished. *Century 21 Masters* now consistently ranks as the number one or two brokerage firms in the entire state of California. It often ranks in the Top Ten in the entire United States. And, this real estate empire is run by a man who will be the first to tell you had horrible balance in his life and business for years and years until he finally figured out what was necessary to turn everything around.

One of the things that he attributes to that turnaround is the realization that he needed to make some big changes. Now, I never actually asked Neil if I could share his wisdom in this book, so Neil, if you are reading this, thank you for the insight all those years ago.

"You are where you are in life because you're okay with it. If you weren't, you'd change?" Truer words were never spoken. As with chapter four, this chapter is going to be a very confrontational and probably a difficult part of the book for some to read. This means it could be the most powerful part of the book to read as well by the way.

Confronting our downfalls, our inefficiencies and our weaknesses in an honest and authentic manner is very difficult, to say the least. It is a blow to our egos and a challenge to our souls. Yet, it is entirely necessary for growth. And in case you didn't know, growth is painful. Go to the gym and lift some weights for a few hours. What do you feel like the next day? Sore as you know what. Do it for a few days and watch your muscles grow. It's painful, and your muscles will ache. But, they'll grow. Growth as a person, in life and business, is just as painful. In fact, it's much more painful because it's not just a certain muscle of the body that hurts. And, the growth is not always as easy to see.

In chapter six, we discussed the importance of tracking which would allow you to understand what you're efficient or inefficient at. Change can happen when you're able to actually see what your strengths and weaknesses are and make adjustments. Those adjustments are the changes. And those changes typically mean that you have to do something new that is outside your comfort zone instead of doing what you would like to do or what you are used to doing. Usually your habits are not good habits, know what I mean?

Making the necessary changes and experiencing the pain of being outside your comfort zone goes back to that amazing Winston Churchill quote from chapter three about not just doing your best but doing what is required. Doing your best is usually fun to try, but doing what is required not so much.

You need to take a good, hard look at your life, your business and at the success or lack thereof that you're having and make some hard choices. You need to make decisions about what changes are necessary. Do you need to wake up earlier each day? Do you need to try harder at certain tasks? Do you need to focus more closely on the here and now? What changes are you going to make so that you can change your life?

"To get what you've never had, you must to do what you've never done." You have to ask yourself what have you never had? What do you want? What have you never done? How are you willing to put yourself out there to make it happen? Take a moment to think about what changes you need to make. .

What can I do that I've never done to get what I've never had?

Great! The thought above and your answer are your new marching orders. You've just identified what it is you need to start doing differently. Of course, now the challenge is to actually do things differently. You must execute the plans, your changes, from the list you just made and not just talk about doing it.

You must ask yourself the question, "Am I okay with where I'm at?" and answer it honestly. In some parts of your life, the answer to that is yes. However, in some parts of your life, the answer to that is no. The same will go for your business.

Some of the things in life and business you find that you're okay with, and some you're not. The trick is to be honest with yourself. You must confront reality and authentically look at where you are now in order to be able to have a genuine answer about changes you need to make no matter how difficult, scary, or painful. You're not talking about what changes you want to make. You're talking about what changes you will have to make; The changes that are required for you to have success.

Since you've identified the changes you are going to be making, it's time to go back to the previous chapter covering *The Pyramid* and incorporate those changes. Add those changes so you see them and are reminded of them on a daily basis. Keep them in front of you. Stay focused on them. Continue to chip away at achieving them constantly inch-by-inch, in this game of life.

Notes:

Eight

Failing is the Key to Success

"I have missed more than 9,000 shots in my career. I have lost almost 300 games. On 26 occasions, I have been trusted to take the game-winning shot and I missed. I have failed over and over and over again in my life and that is why I succeed."

Michael Jordan

As I was writing this chapter, I struggled with the concept of how to best get across to you how failure leads to success. It's easy thing to say, but I know when it's you having to decide whether or not to take action, and possibly fail, those words are not quite so easy to digest. So I decided the best way to get the point across would be to share several amazing stories of success with you. Each of these stories has more than it's fair share of failures along the way. It's stories like these that I believe best teach us how important a role failure plays in success. Lets start with Michael Jordan.

Michael Jordan was cut from his high school basketball team, not because he was a discipline problem and not because he didn't have the grades. He was cut from the team because he did not possess the skills to make the team. Imagine that! Considered to be the greatest basketball player of all time in the history of the NBA, and at one point he did not possess the skills to play on his high school basketball team.

He was a gifted athlete and his talents were God-given. That's what made him the greatest ever they say. However, if that were the case, don't you think he would have made his high school basketball team? Have you ever seen high school basketball players? Some of them are quite good but they, on a whole, are not exactly the most impressive bunch of God-given gifted players. What does that tell us? If Michael Jordan couldn't make that team in high school, he couldn't have had that much God-given talent. Yet, he became the greatest basketball player in the history of mankind? How? He worked his tail off. He worked and he worked and then he worked some more.

Most people don't know this about Michael Jordan, but he was considered very disciplined. According to his coaches and teammates, he was the most disciplined person they had ever met. He had the highest level of focus that they had ever seen. In perfecting his skills, he was more dedicated than anyone else. Do people use those types of words to describe you?

However, they say his biggest strength was he was simply not afraid to fail. He was not afraid to fail because he understood failure was an integral part of success. He believed failure was a necessary component. He realized that without putting himself out there to risk failing all the time he was not giving himself the opportunity to succeed very often.

Take a look at your life. How often did you miss opportunities because you were afraid of taking a chance? Were you afraid you might fall flat on your face and fail? How often did you miss the golden opportunity because you were afraid of what would happen if it didn't work? Go back a couple of chapters and read the quote from Will Smith about fear, and ask is it fear or is it danger? Remember, fear is not real. Fear of failure is so common and it is so powerful, but it is not real. How do you control the fear? How do you overcome the fear? How do you push through the fear? On the other side of fear lies success. On the other side of whatever you are afraid of lies the thing you want. So how are you going to get there?

The late, great Nelson Mandela said this. "Our deepest fear is not that we are inadequate. Our deepest fear is that we are powerful beyond measure. It is our light, not our darkness that most frightens us. We ask ourselves, 'Who am I to be brilliant, gorgeous, talented and fabulous?' Actually, who are you not to be? You are a child of God. Your playing small does not serve the world. There is nothing enlightened about shrinking so that other people will not feel insecure around you. We are all meant to shine, as children do. We were born to make manifest the glory of God that is within us. It is not just in some of us; it is in everyone, and as we let our own light shine, we unconsciously give others permission to do the same. As we are liberated from our own fear, our presence automatically liberates others."

Wow! Isn't that an amazing quote? He says our deepest fear is not that we are inadequate but our deepest fear is that we are powerful beyond measure. "Can he really be talking about me?" is what you must be asking yourself right now. Yes, he is talking about all of us.

Let me tell you another story as it was told to me and let's see if you can guess who I am talking about before getting to the part that gives it away.

There was a young black man who lived in Mississippi in the 1930's. Again, this is a true story. This young boy had a stutter. It was a huge stutter. He was made fun of by friends and even his family because his stutter was so bad. It was practically impossible for him to get any words out or for anyone to understand him.

When the young boy was old enough, he began his schooling. Of course, in school, he would stutter and the other children made fun of him. They teased him so much and he was so embarrassed that he decided to give up speaking entirely. He was so afraid of being made fun of that he stopped all verbal communication. That's right; No speaking at all, ever. Not at school. Not at home. Not to his parents. Not to friends. Zero speaking. He didn't speak for eight years. Imagine, eight years of not talking.

However, this boy was smart. He was really smart. As he moved through elementary school and through middle school, he was considered a pretty good student who just didn't speak. Then he got to high school. An English teacher noticed how incredibly gifted this young man was academically and how much it was hurting him by not speaking. The English teacher's name was Donald Crouch. He took this young man under his wing and he began to mentor him and coach him on how to control his stutter.

Imagine, eight years of not talking. Remember, when he did talk, the speech was so bad that everybody laughed at him and made fun of him. Imagine him being so afraid of the failure of speaking wrong that he didn't speak at all. Yet, finally, somebody offered him help because that person saw something special in him, something that no one else had ever seen or recognized. What if that was you? The young man had a choice to make. We sometimes have choices to make. He could either move forward and take advantage of the new opportunity being presented to him and leave his comfort zone of no talking; Or he could stay in his comfort zone and continue to not speak and miss the opportunity. He chose correctly. He decided to get out of his comfort zone and face his fear of failure. Are you able to get out of your comfort zone and face your fears?

Crouch noticed all sorts of things that most never realized about controlling stutters back at the beginning of the century. Things like vocabulary trigger words, problem alphabetic letters and a poetic rhythm of speech. His recognition of the issues ultimately helped this young man get to the point where he began to speak again and eventually speak without a stutter.

The young man faced his fear, overcame his fear, and took advantage of the opportunity in spite of his fear. And it worked. He succeeded. After eight years of silence, he was speaking again.

After graduating from high school the young man was accepted to the University of Michigan, one of the Nation's top universities, majoring in Pre-Med. Of course, life happens and the young man decided to take a break from his studies and join the Army for the Korean War. He became an Army Ranger. Imagine this young man from Mississippi who didn't talk for eight years now a Ranger leading men in battle. After the war, he decided not to go back to college. Instead, he found that he had a love of performing, so he began to take acting classes. Isn't it simply incredible that someone who was too afraid to talk to even his family members was taking acting classes to perform in front of audiences? How's that for overcoming fear of failure?

In case you didn't know it, public speaking is the number one fear of most people. When polls are conducted of what people are most afraid of, public speaking is always at the top. Even more amazing is what comes in at number two; Death. Apparently, most people would rather die than have to speak in front of a group of people.

After all the lessons from high school, college, Korea, acting and life in general, eventually, the man hit the big time. His voice, which had no stutter, became probably the most recognizable and famous voice in the world. Know who it is yet? It was used for characters like Darth Vader in *Star Wars* and Mufasa in *The Lion King*. That's right, we're talking about James Earl Jones.

But, he didn't become who he is today because of a God-given talent or natural gifts. Quite the opposite. His story of success is one of adversity, perseverance, and facing his fears to grab on to an opportunity. Like Michael Jordan, he worked and worked and then worked some more.

Everything you ever wanted is out there. If you just step outside your comfort zone and go get it. Dream big. Try the impossible. Don't be afraid to fail. And if you do fail, just keep trying. If you fail again, you try again. Fail again, try again. I love the saying, "It's impossible to beat someone who doesn't give up." Take risks. Be bold. Be fearless. Don't shrink away from fears. Instead, challenge them, attack them, and beat them back.

Success might only be one more failure away. What if you had tried just one more time? What's more important? Success or the failure you might experience along the way while getting there? Do you want success so badly that failure along the way is irrelevant so long as you achieve success in the end? You can conquer your fears. You can succeed. You can have anything you want in this life.

Notes:

Nine

If I Could Do It All Over

"I took at good, long hard look at what I'd do if I could do it all again."

Tim McGraw

There's a country music song I really enjoy listening to sometimes to get some perspective. It's by Tim McGraw, *Live Like You Were Dying*. This song is full of life lessons and advice for me. One is "I loved deeper, spoke sweeter, and gave forgiveness that I'd been denying." Another is, "I was finally the husband that most the time I wasn't, and I became a friend a friend would like to have." And a third, "I took a good, long, hard look at what I'd do if I could do it all again." I really love that line the most.

So, if I could do it all again, what would I do differently? In the first chapter, I described how in 2007 my life and business was crumbling. But I have not explained why. What happened you've probably wondered? Why the change? How did things get so bad? So, here is that story.

My life was crumbling because of my pending divorce and that my soon-to-be ex-wife was moving a few hours away with my three sons. Add in the fact my three sons hardly knew me, even when we did live together. Easy to see why I would describe that as crumbling, right?

I decided to sell my businesses, retire and start to be a better father. This would enable me to move closer to them in Newport Beach and spend more time with them. I had an opportunity to sell and cash out and took it. Retired at age 35 a multimillionaire or at least that was my thought. It turns out I was wrong, very wrong.

My retirement was short lived. Somehow, I did not clearly understand retirement income or more importantly the expenses. I learned the hard way if you continue to spend the same way as when you had actual income you're going to run out of money pretty quickly. Couple that with the fact that I didn't just spend money the same way; I spent money even faster because I wasn't working. That meant I had a lot more time to have a lot more fun. Poor planning and a very poor financial discipline had led me to bankruptcy when just a couple years before I was set for life.

You already know some of the ups and downs from 2007 through the beginning of 2011 when things started to change for me once I'd regained control of my mindset and emotions. Here are a few bits and pieces I have not already shared.

Although my business was non-existent and my finances were a disaster, I was spending a lot more time with my sons, which was fantastic. I was coaching their sporting teams. I was their Cub Scout den leader. I attended all their school events and even volunteered weekly in their classrooms. That part was a bit weird, since it was just me and a bunch of moms, but the kids loved it so I loved it. My personal life was doing much better but financially the hole I was digging continued to get deeper and deeper. Still, I had no balance.

Another tidbit; after my divorce, I had another relationship which resulted in my beautiful daughter, McKenna. However, the relationship with her mom had also blown up. I was again a single man, dead broke, with four children from two different women, but I was being an involved dad.

However, being an involved dad was only half the job. I was failing at the other half. You see, involved, but broke, unfortunately means the kids suffer somewhat too. If they wanted to do something, I couldn't always afford it. For instance broke doesn't cover the fees to participate in a season of soccer, attend a summer church camp, or buy their school photos. Embarrassed, I had to turn to my parents and my brother for help with these kinds of expenses. Broke doesn't help during birthdays or Christmas. But again, my family did. Particularly difficult was the fact the two older boys, Sawyer and Jonah, were old enough to remember what it was like just a few years earlier when money was no issue. I would overhear them sometimes talking to each other and saying things like, "Do you remember when we used to be rich and we could do those things, and we could buy that stuff?" It was really difficult to hear.

While my business life and finances didn't begin to improve until 2011, on the personal side I was still making progress and I did experience some balance. And a wonderful thing happened. I met the woman who would later become my wife. To say she was instrumental in helping me get my life back on track would be the understatement of all-time.

Back to the song lyrics, "Finally I was the husband that most the time I wasn't." I had met a beautiful, caring and compassionate soul-mate, Melody. I set my mind to this time I was going to get it right.

"I became a friend a friend would like to have." At the beginning of this book, I mentioned that some of my friends turned out to not be my friends when I needed them. Most of my friends today have been with me through the good and the bad. And I try to be that sort of a friend to them. Ron Gifford, from Ocean City, New Jersey, has been one of those friends at my side through good and bad. There's another old saying I like, "If you were absent during my struggle don't expect to be present during my success." My friends know they can count on me no matter what. They know that I'll be there regardless. Ron is one of those friends I know I can count on no matter what and he knows he can count on me as well.

"I took a good, long, hard look at what I'd do if I could do it all again." So, if I could do it all again, what would I do differently? What changes would I make? If I could go back and do it all again, the outcome would obviously be different. And the experiences along the way would be different. And the things learned would be different. And because of all those differences, I'm not sure that given the chance to go back would I make any changes. Because, oddly enough, if I went back and made changes to correct the errors, I'd be a different person today. And I don't want that. I like the person I am today. It would have been easier, sure, but if I had made changes, I wouldn't have learned all the lessons along the way. I ask myself all the time what sort of ripple effect would be created by simply changing one of the uncomfortable lessons. I certainly wouldn't have the level of appreciation and gratitude that I now have without all the failures and lessons. I certainly wouldn't have the discipline I have developed. I believe the mistakes I made and my failures were necessary steps and wouldn't trade them now for anything easier.

It's important to learn from the lessons along the way. Failures are supposed to teach us something. Let's not waste the lesson. I didn't go through all the failures and pain to not learn from them and simply continue to repeat my mistakes. Each and every failure acted as a guidepost for me to follow in the right direction in the future. Failures were just speed bumps along the way. They didn't stop me. They taught me. Each and every time we fail in the future we must continue to learn and adjust. You must never forget that going through the trials and tribulations is necessary. You must never forget that what you learn from tough times is a necessary piece of the puzzle in order to be truly successful.

Notes:

Ten

The Book That Changed My Life

"Money is plentiful for those who understand the simple rules of its acquisition."

The Richest Man in Babylon

Over the past few years I had started spending tons of quality time with my children. I had started to get my mindset under control. I started a new amazing relationship with Melody. Then in 2011, things started to turn for the better financially a bit.

That's when I came across a book that I had heard of, but had never gotten around to reading, *The Richest Man in Babylon* by George S. Clason. It literally changed my life.

I've already mentioned that old saying that we overestimate what we can accomplish in one year, and underestimate what we can accomplish in five. Let's start by talking about that first year.

I was embroiled in a custody battle for my daughter. Thank goodness, that was never an issue with my three sons. The boy's mother and I were always very clear that we would split time equitably in some fashion, and the monthly financial obligations wouldn't change because of it, which makes custody a lot easier to resolve for the sake of the kids.

Unfortunately, with the second relationship, that wasn't the case and I spent over a year in court before winning joint custody of my daughter. I was not able to afford an attorney to go to the custody hearings so I did all the legal paperwork myself. I appeared in family court twenty-seven times and argued with the other attorney in front of the judge. It was quite a learning lesson. Being able to achieve what I did in the courtroom is one of my proudest moments.

In that first year, I was still late on my rent every month. I still couldn't pay for all of my kids' activities and was having to borrow money. At this point, I didn't even have a car, and had borrowed one for transportation purposes. No car. Can you imagine? Pretty broke, right? My retirement accounts were completely wiped out. My homes were all foreclosed. I was even selling personal belongings in order to pay some of my monthly bills. Doesn't sound like much progress in the first year, does it? But it was. I was coaching. I had income. My mindset was getting better. I was turning the corner.

You've got to ask yourself why the heck Melody would want to get involved with a man in that situation. I certainly do, almost every day. And each and every day all these years later I still thank my lucky stars for the blessing I received in her.

Being able to lean on Melody for support in that first year is, I believe, one of the things that led to completely turning my life around. She was my foundation. She took some of the weight off my shoulders so I didn't feel like Atlas holding the weight of the world on my shoulders. She was carrying some of the weight for me. She believed in me and the way that she pushed me to beat back the adversity I was facing was incredible.

At this point, we were in complete survival mode. Melody had drained her 401(k) and all bank accounts keeping us afloat. She had gotten rid of her Mercedes. She had gone all-in on us.

How broke? Once a month we went to the dollar movie theater, bought a few dollar-hot dogs and shared a two-dollar coke for a total of ten dollars all-in for our once a month date. And interestingly enough, we were very happy. They are right. Money doesn't buy happiness. However, money sure does make it easier.

There are a few things that I want to mention before talking about the changes that began to occur as 2011 progressed. Previous years taught us to appreciate the little things. It was a lesson for us to be grateful for all the things that we had in our lives, day-in and day-out, which we didn't necessarily recognize before, but were extremely special. Those years taught us humility. Those years taught us discipline. The discipline was forced upon us because we couldn't spend money simply because there wasn't any. But, it was still a discipline that was earned and learned the hard way. It taught us graciousness, humility, and appreciation. Those lessons would be invaluable as things started to get better for us in 2011 and great for us in 2012.

Now, to be clear, I am not a financial analyst or a personal wealth advisor, or anything of the kind. Obviously, since I wasted millions of dollars. But, I will tell you that the lessons learned in the book *The Richest Man in Babylon* are tried and true methods for building wealth. I've told you about our budget. Great dad but dead broke. I've told you not to overestimate what you can do in one year or underestimate what you can do in five years. Now let me tell you what happened after that first year in 2011.

The difference between year one in 2011 and year six in 2016 in my life has been truly amazing. First, we don't have to share a car anymore. Thank goodness! We each own our car outright so we are not indebted to any car company with a monthly payment. Actually, we have no debt other than real estate. No credit card balances. No installment payments of any sort. Also, we're no longer late on our rent payments. In fact, we no longer rent because we've bought a house. While we don't live in a multi-million dollar mansion on a lake, we do live in a million dollar home in an incredible community. Our parents no longer have to support the extracurricular activities for the children. Instead, we've been able to hire world-class professional athletes, past Olympians, and World Champions to personally coach them in their individual chosen sports to help them excel.

The dollar movies with the one-dollar hot dogs and shared two-dollar sodas are actually still one of our favorite things to do as a couple. However, now we're able to do so much more. Vacations have included trips around the world to walk on The Great Wall of China in Beijing; dinner in the Eiffel Tower in Paris; shopping in the Grand Bazaar in Istanbul; standing in the shadows of the Great Pyramids on the Giza Plateau of Egypt. And those are not even a third of the trips we been blessed to have taken.

Our entire life today has changed financially. We're not spending all that we make as we were before. Actually, we're not even spending half of it, because we now have financial discipline. We've learned the hard lessons and we've forced ourselves to do it better this time.

How did we do it? By reading a book? That's certainly part of it, but by no means all of it. That's just how it started. The book is set in Ancient Babylon and is a parable-style story of financial lessons and disciplines that we should all learn and follow. Many we've probably heard as advice from our parents growing up, but we've never actually followed the advice. You know what? Our parents were right and we were wrong. Mom and Dad, I want to make sure you re-read that last sentence.

So, we read the book. More importantly, we began to implement the lessons from the book. I'm not going to ruin the story for you. Telling you about the book in a couple of paragraphs is not going to be enough. You need to go and read the one hundred and eighty-nine page book. Yes, it's only one hundred and eighty-nine pages. It'll only take you a night or two. It's a very easy read. It's like a storybook, not a textbook. Pick it up, read it, and begin to implement and execute what it tells you to do. Once we began to follow the lessons learned from it's pages we were soon able to do more, save more, invest more and live more.

Mind you, I am making nowhere near the amount of money I used to make. I am only making a fraction of what I used to make in gross income, yet the net income to me, and money being saved and invested and put away correctly is more than I'd ever managed to do before. That's incredible isn't it? If you could accomplish that, do you think your life would be better? Say, "Yes." So, how do you do it? First, you read the book. Then, and this isn't brain surgery guys and gals, you do what the book says. You begin to actually implement it's very, very simple lessons.

I'm asked all the time what books would I recommend reading. Without a doubt, the number one book I always recommend to everyone whenever I'm asked is *The Richest Man in Babylon*. I hope I'm making this abundantly clear to you that the first thing you should do when putting the book down is buy your own copy of it right away.

A past client of mine named Jeff Chiate from Orange County, California once shared this thought with me. He told me there's a difference between being rich and being wealthy. His definition of those two was this. "Being rich means you can go anywhere, buy anything and do anything you want, whenever you want, but you have to keep working to afford it. Being wealthy is being able to go anywhere, buy anything and do anything you want and you don't have to work to pay for it." I think those are pretty good definitions, however, I've changed them just a bit over the years.

I still completely agree with his definition of rich. We can do all those things but we still have to grind and continue to work our tails off to keep the lifestyle going. I think that's somebody who's living rich, or we would look at as a rich person. So how has my definition of wealthy changed over the years?

I believe a wealthy person is someone who doesn't necessarily do as much, spend as much, or appear as a rich as they are because their other values in life are more developed. It's not just about buying the newest shiny car or multi-million dollar home on the lake. They might have the same amount as money as a rich person. They might still have to work too. But what makes them wealthy is much more than just how much they can spend. The rich spend. The wealthy? The difference? It's in their mindset. The wealthy are gracious. The wealthy are humble. I think a rich person takes things for granted and is all flash. I think a wealthy person is someone who lives a life of not only of things, but also of substance.

Those are just my definitions. I challenge you to come up with your own. What do you consider to be rich? What do you consider to be wealthy? What's the difference between the two? Which one do you want to be? What are you trying to become? Who are you trying to emulate? What is it, exactly, that you want to accomplish? Use the following page to formulate your own thoughts on these questions.

Notes:

Eleven

Taking Action

"You might want to decide fast. We live in a dangerous world. If you see a chance to be happy, you have to fight for it, so later you have no regrets."

Ilona Andrews

The quote above is pretty impressive, is it not? Decide quickly. As we've talked about in previous chapters, sometimes we don't take action because we're afraid of getting it wrong. We're afraid of failing, fear freezes us, and we make no forward progress. Make a decision, good or bad, right or wrong. Live with it. If it didn't work, try it again the next time a different way.

When you're feeling the emotion, the spark, you must take action. When you have that burning feeling deep inside of you, that feeling of desire to accomplish something, you must take action.

How often have I sat at my desk, and suddenly thought to myself, "Oh my gosh, this is brilliant. I think I have a great idea for something?" We've all had those moments. We've thought about them, dreamed about them, maybe even planned for them just a little, and then done nothing else with them? I have. We all have.

I've probably done that over the course of my life a couple of hundred times if not a thousand times. Having great ideas is obviously a component to success, but executing on those ideas, actually doing something about them, that's what will separate us from 99 percent of the population. It takes work and because it might not work and we might fail, we're afraid to take that risk.

A favorite quote of mine is from the John Galt character in Ayn Rand's *Atlas Shrugged*. He says, "Do not let your fire go out, spark by irreplaceable spark in the hopeless swamps of the not-quite, the not-yet, and the not-at-all. Do not let the hero in your soul perish in lonely frustration for the life you deserved and have never been able to reach. The world you desire can be won. It exists. It is real. It is possible. It's yours."

That passage really resonates with me. Our ideas are like fires burning within us. We can't allow them to go out spark by spark. We all have heroes inside of us. We can't let our heroes die because we never let them out to be. What you want is out there and it is possible. You simply have to be willing to do what is necessary to get it. It does exist and it is real and it is possible. How badly do you want it?

By the way, earlier I mentioned *The Richest Man in Babylon* as being my number one suggested book to read. *Atlas Shrugged* is number two.

Ask yourself a question. How great is that going to be if you succeed? What is that going to mean in your life and to your family and to your loved ones? Could it change your world? The answer is always, yes.

Next question. If you fail, how much worse will it make your life than it already is? Interestingly, the answer is probably not much. If you go on this bold adventure, and take these great risks and execute on the plans that you've come up with and they don't work out, what has it cost you? It might cost you a tiny bit of time. It might cost you a tiny bit of money. It might cost you a blow to your ego. Ultimately, it's not going to impact your life all that much. Tomorrow will be just like today.

But if it works! Then what? Oh the changes you would see, right?

My old mentor Tim Wood used to say, "Emotion makes them act; logic makes them think." We need to do a better job of taking advantage of our emotions and taking action. When we're excited about something we must actually start to take action and work towards it and make progress on it. That's when we can move mountains.

The problem is we get the great idea and then we don't do anything with it. Then, two weeks later, we go back to the great idea but we're not excited about it any more. We've lost the emotion, the spark, so we don't do anything with it. Ralph Waldo Emerson's quote is very true: "Nothing great was ever achieved without enthusiasm." When you're feeling pumped up and inspired, act. When you're feeling that energy course through your veins, you've got to do something about it. Act.

I know, you're busy. The people who come up with the great ideas they were busy too, but they still found time to work on executing their plans and to do something about them. They got up earlier, they stayed up later, and they gave up watching so much TV. I guarantee sacrifices were made along the way. Show me a successful person who has never had to sacrifice a little bit of fun to achieve success, and you will have shown me the impossible.

I have dozens of personal stories about times I have had a great idea and took no action and lost it, being too busy, or lazy, to get to it. I also have dozens of personal stories about times I have had a great idea and took action and it turned out to not be such a great idea after all and it failed. And finally, I have dozens of personal stories about times I have had a great idea and took action and it turned out to be amazing for me and my family.

Do you know which ones I think about the most? It's the ideas that I did nothing with. I constantly regret not having taken the chance to do something with a great idea. When I tried and I failed, I moved on with a lesson learned. No big deal. Next. Then, of course, there are my successes. I don't think much about them. I tried it. It worked. I'm living a better life because of it. Next. It's the ideas that I did nothing with which gnaws at me. What if I had taken action? What if the ideas had worked out as great as I thought? If they'd failed, no biggie. But man, if they had worked! How could those ideas have changed my life? I'll never know.

Make a promise to yourself; The next time you have a great idea that you're going to actually do something about it. Commit to yourself that when something comes up you won't be afraid to try it and you won't be afraid to fail at it.

Notes:

Twelve

Be Grateful

"Be thankful for what you have, you'll end up having more. If you concentrate on what you don't have you will never, ever have enough."

Oprah Winfrey

It is very easy to be caught up in things going on around us, what we are trying to accomplish, what we are trying to obtain, and how we are trying to succeed. Along the way, we forget about all the good things that have already happened to us and all the positive things that have occurred. We tend to only focus on what we think our future should look like. We get tunnel vision and don't see life in our peripheral. Remember, living is the six inches in front of our face. It's not next year. It's now.

It took me years and years to recognize all the fantastic things I had around me and to truly be grateful for them. I was so busy trying to get more I had never stopped to notice all that I had. Today, I understand how much better I have it than I did in the past. Don't get me wrong, climbing the ladder of success and moving up and up and up is a great thing. We just need to make sure we're doing it proportionally, in both business and life. Along the way we need to be grateful for the steps we've taken, appreciating how far we've come.

More than a decade ago I was first made aware of being grateful by a gentleman, named John Alexandrov. I was participating in a two-day mastermind meeting in Orlando, Florida and he was the guest speaker. He shared with us his book, *Affirmations of Wealth*. In the few hours we spent listening to him speak I became aware that he was probably the most gracious and humble man I had ever met. As the audience peppered him with questions, the underlying tone of everything he said was to be grateful for all that we had. At the time, I was probably in my early thirties. And I kid you not, honest to God, I'd never heard anybody say that. Maybe someone had said it, but I'd never heard it. I had only heard do more, get more, be more, keep going, strive to be the best, conquer the world. And that's what I was trying to do. I'd heard the old saying to make sure you take the time to stop and smell the roses, but I'd never really had it sink in before. If you have not read the book, and it's sort of a workbook by the way, I suggest you pick up your own copy. Be grateful. What a simple message. I had no idea how life changing it could be.

Years later, I was finally learning how to be grateful, thankful and appreciative. It changed the way others perceived me when I started to behave differently and that's a good thing. I've mentioned earlier in these pages about being perceived as a jerk at one point in my life. When I started to realize all that I had and be grateful for it, it also increased my humility at the same time. And you know what I learned? Someone who is grateful and humble is someone who is hard to not like.

A friend, Matthew Ferry, from Newport Beach, California shared one of my all time favorite quotes by Johann Wolfgang von Goethe.

"Until one is committed, there is hesitancy, the chance to draw back. Always ineffectiveness. Concerning all acts of initiative (and creation), there is an elementary truth the ignorance of which kills countless ideas and splendid plans. The moment one definitely commits oneself, then Providence moves too. All sorts of things occur to help one that would never otherwise have occurred. A whole stream of events issues from the decision, raising in one's favor all manner of unforeseen incidents and meetings and material assistance, which no man could have dreamed would have come his way. Whatever you can do, or dream you can do, begin it. Boldness has genius, power, and magic in it. Only engage and the mind grows heated. Simply begin and the task will be completed."

To be honest, this quote could have been used in several different chapters in this book. It touches on mindset (multiple chapters); providence (this chapter); taking action (chapter 11); the list goes on and on. I could practically write an entire book on just this quote breaking down its powerful message sentence-by-sentence, chapter-by-chapter. However, I chose to share this quote in this chapter because of the part about providence.

To me, providence is when it seems like the universe is aligning to say "thank you." Have you ever had that happen? When it seems like everything is going your way and you've run into a crazy amount of good luck? That's providence.

Couple those opportunities we are given with a great work ethic and execution of plans and they start to breed success, gratefulness and humility. That's an insanely likeable person we all aspire to become, correct? And that snowball effect all begins with recognizing and being grateful for what we have.

Remember, being grateful for what we have doesn't mean we don't have dreams to have more. It's all about balance.

"It's that picture in our heads of what it's supposed to be like that screws us up the most." What a great reminder. I have this quote on a banner that I use quite often when I'm travelling to speak. We all have this picture in our heads of what it supposed to be like, don't we? We have this idea of how it is supposed to be, right? And is it usually, or even ever, like our fantasy picture? Is our daydream of how we want it to happen reality or fiction? I believe that the fictional picture in our head screws up the reality in our lives.

Don't get me wrong, dreaming big is ok. It's fun. And it's important. But let's make sure our dreams are based in reality. Do you want a million dollars in the bank, a mansion, a nice car and no debt? Fantastic! Go out and make it happen. But, we need to make sure your plan to do it is based in the real world. To accomplish all of those things you'd better have a picture in your head of hard work, long days and lots of sacrifices. It's not going to happen by delegating all the hard work to a team. It's not going to happen by working from 9 am until 5 pm Monday through Friday with an hour off for lunch. It's going to happen if you make it happen. It won't just happen because you want it to. You can make it happen with your blood, sweat and tears.

Notes:

Thirteen

The Wrap Up

"All our dreams can come true if we have the courage to pursue them."

Walt Disney

I would like to say congratulations on making it to the last chapter of the book. Believe it or not, statistically, more books are started and not finished than are actually finished. So again, congratulations on setting yourself apart from the rest by completing something you've started. I would also like to express my sincere gratitude for you taking time out of your busy life to consider what I had to share and to giving me the opportunity to possibly help in some way.

Writing this book and getting my thoughts and ideas on paper in some sort of intelligible order was the hard part for me. Now comes the hard part for you. How are you going to take the lessons learned and put them into practice? That's always the challenge. "People" go to seminars and they come back fired up, but they don't do anything with the information they got while they were there. "People" read books and get lots of ideas, but don't know how to take those ideas and do anything to change their lives or to change what they do on a daily basis. But you are not just "people". What they do does not dictate what you will do. You now have a blueprint to follow. You know to take action when the emotion is hot. You know that failure is not to be feared, but is a vital piece of the puzzle to becoming successful. And you know that balance is the key.

So now, you begin a new journey. Reading the book was the easy part. Doing what you are supposed to do is going to be the hard part. How do you do it? Simple. How do you eat an elephant? That's right, one bite at a time.

Remember from chapter ten, I discussed that we always overestimate what we can accomplish in one year and underestimate what we can accomplish in five. That goes for this book. Hopefully, as you went through the book you made some notes and you underlined some important parts.

What I would encourage you to do now is to go back through the book, chapter-by-chapter, and pull out the three most important things in every chapter. Just three. Even if there is four, five or six I'm going to ask you to limit it to just three. Once you've completed those three things that were the most important, by all means, go back and pick a fourth, a fifth, or even a sixth. A poor plan is to list everything and be so overwhelmed that you're unable to start. Just pick the top three things in each chapter. Work on achieving them. Then you can consider going back for more.

Think about this. When you achieve the top three things you got out of each chapter you'll have over 30 powerful ideas completed. And when those 30 things are completed I guarantee your life will be so much different, for the better. The level of success you are having will be so much higher. The balance will be so much better.

Let's review chapter two. What really stuck out to you as we discussed the fear of failure? In chapter three, what parts of the mindset gym are you going to implement? In chapter four, have you already played the worst-case scenario game? Or have you been putting it off because of how painful it is? In chapter five, life's a game of inches. It's constant small steps towards progress. How are you going to do that? In chapter six, we covered *The Pyramid* and goal planning. Have you started filling it in? Chapter-by-chapter, get to work.

Taking the information in this book and putting it all into practice is going to be a huge task. As I have already said, "I didn't say it was going to be easy. I said it was going to be worth it." As Walt Disney said, "Have the courage to pursue your dreams." Obliterate your fear of failure. Embrace what your life and business can look like and how successful they can both be in balance with each other. It's all out there for you to take. It's just a matter of whether or not you're going to do what's necessary to take it. I wish you well on this journey. Be brave, be confident, and most of all, be fearless.

Notes:

Receive your free one-week sample of the *Daily Victory Log* and Dan's personal *Pyramid* by going to the author's website.

www.ByDanSmith.com

27067305R00074

Made in the USA
Columbia, SC
20 September 2018